7 Hearts & 3 Verses

Sanjeevani Srivastava

BookLeaf
Publishing

India | USA | UK

Made with ❤ on the BookLeaf Publishing Platform

www.bookleafpub.in

www.bookleafpub.com

Dedication

To all those with a wild imagination & fantasies yet to realize.

Preface

Dear Reader,
Something about this book must have made you want to open it, and thus I'm beyond excited to introduce you to my book, 7 *Hearts & 3 Verses*. This collection is a celebration of emotions, dreams, and reflections, all intertwined with 7 of my most beloved themes. Each theme features 3 carefully crafted poems, offering a glimpse into different facets of life, love, and imagination.

Within these pages, you'll find yourself traveling through worlds both real and mythical. From the captivating allure of mystical creatures to the empowering strength of women, each poem is a doorway to a story or feeling that resonates deeply with me. Love, in its many forms—both joyous and heartbreaking—takes its place alongside the beauty of nature and the rhythm of the seasons.

Poetry, for me, is not just about words; it's about connection. With every verse, I hope to bring you closer to experiences that are universal yet deeply personal. Each poem is a piece of my heart, woven with words that I hope resonate with yours.

Whether you're seeking solace, adventure, or a quiet moment to reflect, I hope this book becomes a companion for your thoughts and dreams. Every poem has a story, but it's incomplete until you bring your own perspective to it.

So, let's embark on this journey together—one verse, one emotion, and one connection at a time. May you find as much magic in reading these poems as I did in writing them.

With love and gratitude,
Sanjeevani Srivastava

Acknowledgements

This book is the culmination of countless moments of inspiration, reflection, and encouragement, and I am deeply grateful to everyone who has supported me along the way.

To my family, your constant encouragement and belief in my creative pursuits have been my foundation. To my friends, thank you for being my sounding board and for offering feedback that has shaped this collection into something I'm proud to share.

To my readers, you are the heart of this journey. These poems were written with the hope of sparking emotions, thoughts, and connections, and I am endlessly thankful for your time and openness to them.

Finally, I want to acknowledge the experiences, dreams, and quiet musings that have inspired these pages. This collection wouldn't exist without them.

Gratefully,
Sanjeevani Srivastava

1. For the lovers:
I. An Unforeseen-Lovely Sight

He saw someone today,
Coming out of the compound,
A beautiful floral attire,
And a smile so profound.

Though far, every bit was seen,
From the way she backed the hair from her face,
To the way the sun glimmered in her eyes,
Thinking it must've been almost as blessed as he who
saw her grace.

He noticed the way it lighted her,
When she saw a friend,
He observed every detail as she spoke,
Even those that *she* never did.

She saw someone today,
Leanly sitting against his bike,
An Onyx shirt, white-patched,
Which she still seems to like.

Pretending to never look,
Was one of her beloved schemes,
But she did see every bit,
Even the way he sat upright, wanting to learn his
dreams.

Even when she saw her friend,
Her eyes wanted elsewhere,
But never saw each other after,
For them so little could be spared.

II. A Love Like This

You seem a bit too good, too good to be true.
Like stars painting wishes on midnight's blue.

Every time we talk, there enters a peculiar silent
association,
But even that silence between us feels like a
conversation.

You probably never saw me, the way I looked at you,
Because it always felt as if my best parts were in you.

I do see you on streets, in places I really love,
Then make scenarios in my head that I know would
never work.

Even the faintest eye- contacts, seemed like the worlds
colliding,
Every walkway you tread on, felt enhanced by your
light.

Every question you'd throw at me, my *heart* would
process it first,
And in the middle of my answers my voice always
stuttered noticeably.

That didn't rhyme,I know,
But does it have to though?
As that lack of rhyme had personified my feelings about
you.

I do not honestly care, if our feelings aren't mutual,
You're lucky I dwell on memories rather than on person
or things factual.

But I would tell you how special I would feel,
If you'd maybe, just maybe, be more than a memory.

III. A Lover's Heart.

She was prettiest girl he had ever seen,
Though as pretty as the others,
But she had something in her,
That made him a lover.

He never looked at someone,
With such delicacies to discover,
But he saw her eyes- charcoal black,
Suddenly his favourite colour.

It was as if knew a girl for the first time,
Forgetting all of the past,
Her voice settling in his mind,
And leaving an effect so vast.

How he wished to speak his mind,
But those words were better off unspoken
Yet she had fixed something of his heart,
Something she never had broken.

2. For the Daring Lovers
I. Once By a Riverside

Once by a Riverside he met a lone girl,
Felt a strange warmth, yet a painful hurl.
His heart wanted this company, but his mind opposed,
He didn't want this to be another, love imposed.

He went ahead at last, & felt the most blessed,
He felt this to be the final end of his intensive quest.
She probably loved it too, he could see it in her eyes,
He saw the stars in them, as if he'd never seen the skies.

They saw each other everyday, once by the riverside,
She seemed sicker ahead, but he was there to confide.
Never opened his heart to her, afraid to ruin what they
had,
But didn't know beautiful things could end as something
bad.

He tells his friends about her, & they just laugh it out,
But could they know the love that never found a sprout.

'Tis like loving the ocean, yet being afraid to drown,
Wherein you wish to go with the waves,
But even the tides can't reach you out.

Years passed, no talks, he finally took the courage
To make amends past these awkward walks.
Walks through memories, those nostalgic tests,
Through compatible friendships, & through those still
left.

So he went back to the riverside, all week long,
But never saw her again, their love- an unfinished song.
They now only met in memories, the fantasies in his
head,
Their love was like a flower & root,
But what's a pretty flower, with its roots dead.

II. YOU, ME AND HER.

Love, not a feeling, but a person
And for me it was you.
You, whom I can't define in words so few.
You, who were different, than the others who came,
You, who were loving, in a way I had portrayed.

Since day one, I wanted to be your best friend,
Since day one, Had my shoulders for you to attend.
The moment you would talk to me, be it small or big,
I always got butterflies, and a smile on my face.
Not to look pretty, but it was natural,
The feelings you gave me, felt so delusional.

And along came her, who got you smiling like me,
Except, that smile was for her, but was never for me.
She was perfect, like a carved diamond in the sky,
And I was the girl, who saw the time pass by.
If only you had turned your eyes to look elsewhere,
You could've seen me, waiting for you there.

But let me tell you truth that she never cared,
Bout what you would do and the time you spared,
You see, you and I, are just the same,
Be it the type of love or the games we play.
You were with her every time, one like a dove,
I guess then I felt, what was one- sided love.

III. Fortune is Slanted

He was the midnight time,
And she, the twilight sight,
Whilst he was the mountains,
She was the water's tides.

If he lied at one edge of the universe,
She was standing at the other,
Whilst he was a star that just began,
She was already through an explosion.

When he just wanted to settle,
She wished to see the world,
Whilst he wanted to let go,
Her mind was still unfurled.

Both wanted love,
Something to confide to,
They became each other's past,
The past they were still tied to.

3. The Yet Not Known:
I. The Bloody Fairies

They reside in dark places, amongst red berries,
Where sunlight itself recoils,
They spy their hosts, draw them to core,
Those mysterious bloody fairies...

They'll hunt you down till your heart goes sore,
Until you yourself submit,
They show their teeth as sharp as night,
Piercing through your neck.

They look the same for a 1000 years, their face never
varies
They'll lure you by the looks, and you shall be drawn
Into a place where light scares,
Of those luring bloody fairies...

They shan't be invited,
Don't be seduced by their eyes,
For as long as they remain outside,

Your safety is their plight.

They look as ravishing as your blood,
They can hear your heart beat,
But they have no heart, darkness made flesh,
Those bloody fairies are the walking dead...

II. Ocean Carols & Barrels
Fourth

The Ocean carols & barrels fourth,
Through her kin's voices, her own,
Oh so silken and dulcet,
As mesmeric as the Lemurian Stone.

The sailor quests amongst the waves,
Kissed by the lips of the haunting melody,
As he catches those immense rhythms,
My sayings realise- "Curiosity births fatality"

The Ocean carols & barrels fourth,
"Find me, Oh chevalier"
'Twas a sign for a gallant show, a prospect to seize,
So he drifted like all the others,
But if only the sailor was a seer...

He further went, when his angels whispered-
"This trajectory is steep & frail"
But Abyss' devils beckoning him, whispers ceded,

And the voices bore flesh with sapphire orbs,
And a diamond sharp tail.

The Ocean carols & barrels fourth,
The sailor was never seen again,
He faded into the shadows abode,
Who too once had heard the sirens' strain…

III. The Moon's Secret

He is an 18 year old boy,
Who seems as kind as none,
But there is something about him
That makes others want to run.

He sees the moon like none do,
Like it's some symbolism of his love,
Maybe a wound of past,
Or maybe something worse.

They watch him everyday at distance,
He has a charismatic, a fiery sense,
But displays a cold demeanor
Under the moon's incense.

He went one night of full-moon,
Into the densest forests, not knowing he was followed,
And as soon as the canopy revealed the moon,
The follower's mind hollowed.

The man turned into the beast,
That people only know in folklores,
With jarring-claws, mane of wolf,
But the size twice of a boar's.

His hound made the birds fly off,
& probably leave their homes,
But fortune never favoured the follower,
As he was still too slow.

Next day the Sun shown bright,
As the moon kept his secret,
No one could know his story,
As there lived none to tell.

4. . The Divine is a Woman.
I. Tis the Time...

Tis' the 1800s, her life stays limited,
From the man who gave life,
To the man she was given.
She feels detached from the world,
Away from every peril,
Though still she wonders how knowledge could be it.

Tis' the 1900s, she now knows her worth,
She wishes to voice the same, but realizes
There isn't a right for one.
So she begins the search, with fights paralleling her,
Just to paint a vivid life, residing in her imagination.

Tis' the 2000s, the goal realizes,
Yet leaves certain hopes for modern civilization.
She is no more, but looks from above the life she dreamt
of,
Was lived by every girl.

Tis' the 21st century, all has been forgiven,
Yet the mindset hasn't changed,
Even the girls on the streets at night do not feel safe.
This fight never ends, but it shouldn't be called so,
For a woman may exist freely, but hasn't yet lived what
she longed for.

II. The Girl & Her Defiance

The golden of the sunsets was in her eyes,
Her hair flows like the waves of the sea,
Her smile is enough to bless the grieving,
Her face holds beauty of the stars, even the universe
would agree.

With a mind as sharp as the edge of a cliff,
At a height to make the trekkers tremble,
Her knowledge is immense and enough,
To make the men fumble.

Afraid of the strength she keeps,
They coerce her into safety,
She assumed it for the best for her,
And lost the glimmer of her story.

Stunted and diminished,
Her daughters now suffer in silence,
Their mother only tells them stories,
Of the Girl & her Defiance...

III. Morbid Lives.

She seems like magic,
As delicate as light,
She hopes for good of everyone,
And would never want a fight.

But she was already a part of one,
The one she didn't begin,
But being a woman who is right,
Felt almost like a sin.

She is like the water,
Pure, bright and renowned,
But there is a certain depth to her,
Enough to make one drown.

They'd never let her speak,
As her voice was way too strong,
And they'd never let her win,
They knew she'd correct their wrongs.

Ages have passed,
And she had lost the fight,
But her generations in agony,
Are a part of a war so tight.

5. Every Season's Rhythm: I. The Silver-Threaded Heaven

The clouds parade swiftly canopying the wards of earth,
Greyish cotton, feather- light, with air bearing mirth.

All creatures crept into their homes, yet I did step out,
Into the windy, navy hue, when seeds & buds sprout.

As I feel the soil and the sparse grassy seems,
The first drop of rain touches whilst it quickly turns
extreme.

Oh! How we love, the sound of the rain clapping with
the foliage,
The scent of the damp soil, the sight of fog amongst trees
of age.

Though the Sun was hidden as the rain gave it a break,
The drizzly weather mixed with love, lighted every ache.

The time then comes for it to leave & saddened the
meadow,
Yet left a mark to arrive again through the mystical
rainbow.

The months of June & July, of August & September,
When the skyline sheds itself as the
Silver-Threaded Heaven.

II. Winter Floral Divinity.

The frosty season arrives
When the Snowdrop
Eager to blossom,
Blooms in such weather,
That people often address as gloomy...

Its tender petals are so tender
Enough for people to assume
It's light & delicate nature.
O but how it breaks through
The frost of the cold influence.

When Eve became indignant from
The expulsion of Eden,
It became so vast that The Snowdrop
Was summoned to console her.

It gorgeously sets
Against the winter backdrop,
With snow and its buds dancing,

A beauty so exquisite
And much to comprehend
So one can only do nothing but admire.

But beneath that beauteous sight,
Lied a toxic light,
Unconsumable just like love,
As cold as every winter's night.

III. The Summer's Cold Embrace.

The Sun shines the brightest,
And the unbearable heat remains,
While the coasts enjoy the cool breeze,
Temperature additions a few celsius within.

The people turn feeble,
Unable to differentiate if,
Their side-face was shedding water or sweat,
And no clouds were present that sunny day,
As if they just had lost a bet.

Some ran into their homes,
And some to the nearest tree,
To get a shade from the Sun's blaze,
Wished God to put them out of their misery.

Even the birds were heated up,
And the fishes wanted out,
For the waters, lakes & river,

Seemed to boil about.

But along came a cool wind,
Sudden with heroic entry,
And cured the oppressing warmth,
And finally set all free.

6. The Forest to My Heart
I. The Flower I'd Give My Petals to

I hate the way my sister,
Is the first baby I ever had,
Cause' I love her just like I'd my own,
Or maybe even more.

I hate the way I would kill for her,
And that I would bleed too,
I would give her the half
Of the cake I like, and my own half too.

We fight like we are the worst enemies,
Then gossip like best friends,
I hate the way I have to scold her,
And then call her to make amends.

So truly she would be mad at me,
On somethings that I would say,

But she didn't see me crying last night,
When I dreamt of her going away.

I hate the way our parents,
Worry about our "sisterhood',
But they don't know that we know each other,
More than they ever could.

She sees right past my happy eyes,
And right past the pretty smile,
I hate the way she consoles me,
When I've just gone through something vile.

In a crowd full of her fans,
I'd ensure the front seat,
And cheer for her so loud,
But I'd hate for her to miss a beat.

Oh but how I love this beautiful thing,
This beautiful thing between us,
She should know that I would always let her take,
And let myself miss the bus.

II. The Root of My Existence.

I really sometimes wonder,
How my mother's life,
Might've been before me,
And before being considered as someone's wife.

It really sometimes intrigues me,
That she was too once a girl,
A girl with ambitions, with dreams to live,
And she too might've wished to have curls.

It really is so eccentric,
That she had to leave her mother,
The one who gave her life,
Cause' I can't imagine myself without her.

It really seems so forced,
Whenever I ask her her ambitions,
How she'd smile say "Your mother",
Yet mention every single profession.

If there exists a universe,
To live out every dream, realize every imagination,
If she got her chance to be herself,
I'd send her there with no hesitation.

I know that way I wouldn't exist,
But that still feels the least I could do,
Cause' I feel the sacrifices she had made,
Were ten times more worth than my own.

It hurts she can't be here forever,
And that she has a temporary stay,
That's too unfair to someone,
Who molded the games I play.

I love you in every possible way,
Like a best friend, like a daughter of course,
I would make myself worth your every word,
Just guide me as an unseen force.

III. The Tree that Guards My Heart

This man is my first love,
The first to hold my hand,
The one who hears my every word,
Even those who others can't understand.

He held my tiny hands,
Introduced me to the world,
Even his first time as a father,
He treats me like a free bird.

I start going to school,
And I try to get those grades,
Even when they're not so perfect,
His face splatters joy's every shade.

With a blink of an eye, I am a teen,
Know to be annoyed & with a temper,
But he still sees me as his little girl,
And recalls 2nd November.

If I start to stay away,
He'd be the one to miss me,
Even if no one remembers me,
He would ensure to call me daily.

Whenever his eyes tear up,
Something must've been wrong at heart,
Cause' he smiles and cheers me up,
Even when for him the world is falling apart.

I wish to see if his eyes water,
With love & hideous pride,
The look on his face when he looks at me,
When I come as someone's bride.

When the right man arrives in my life,
I would proudly tell him the truth,
That he wasn't the first love I had,
And that truly, it was my Dad.

7. Mysteries Not Ours to Solve.

I. A Blissful Ignorance.

Isn't it so bizarre?
How we assume superiority,
When we might be as tiny as dust
To the ones who truly are superior.
How we declare something to never exist,
Because we ourselves don't hold such courage
To see the things that might gain popularity.

We think we're so special, that we are one of a kind,
But how can that be stated in truth
When we haven't yet seen even our own world
intensively.
How can we be the first, the first to build,
The first to create, to rule, to establish,
When we ourselves give away the possibility
Of an existence of something that was before humanity.

Amongst the trillions of celestials, galaxies, stars
And the infinite cosmos, how can we confidently
State what might be at the universe's edge.
How can we deliberately celebrate humanity
Yet kill our own consciousness to think more than
What is supposed to be thought, to know more
Than what is allowed to be known.

How can we escape the fact
There are things unexplainable, unpredictable,
And the so-called unknown,
When we can't even escape the truth of what is.
How can we remain still when every inch of our mind,
Want us to discover the yet not discovered.

But what if, the undiscovered, doesn't want
To be discovered, what if the unknown,
Must remain that way, what if the unexplainable,
Doesn't wish to explain to us the infinite possibilities.
So how can we declare for things to be illogical,
For things to not make any sense
When the universe isn't obliged to make sense to us.

II. A Soul Divided.

Every second counts, every moment,
Every breath, every sight unbound.
We feel every thing, from pain to joy,
And our eyes are capable to hold tears of both,
Love and suffocation.

But it feels so profoundly unfair,
That we are only given such limited time,
To gain the most ranging experiences.
It's like letting a poor behold a gold lace,
Only to blindfold him for his remainder of life.

We easily complain and crib,
About the little failures,
Not knowing we at least get to feel them.
And we so quickly get encouraged
About the mere moments of happiness,
The small success when they truly become
Unacknowledged by our future-selves.

We can be the strongest & the most dangerous beings,
Yet feel the most sensitive & fragile for
Certain unfortunate things.
This dual existence, a contradicting nature,
I think its time we realize, our uniqueness
Might be common to every existing creature.

III. A Dreamy Reality

What manifests beyond your conscious,
The moment your mind rests,
When that part of your head awakens
Which has recorded every bit of your errands.

You see all you wish to, all that can't be said,
All that you are too afraid to bear,
All that is too overwhelming to be felt,
And all the success you enjoy,
That seems too unrealistic to be achieved.

Is it a form of entertainment for the
Subconscious to enjoy? A beautiful escape
From the dying reality? A warning for
Things ahead? Or a preview of a fortunate event?

It's a place of the most freedom,
To be someone you can't,
To see somebody you're reality doesn't allow,
To hear what your heart desires,

To create your own perfect reality.

It's a place where the false bears the only truth,
Where the fictional suddenly exists,
Where you can control the uncontrollable,
Where the infinity seems definite.

How powerful must be this human mind!
That knows what lies beneath the soul,
The most hidden desires even from you,
And shows the picture if that wish may turn true.